GRANDPARENTS SONG

Sheila Hamanaka

HarperCollinsPublishers

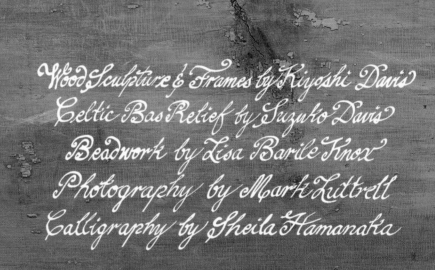

Wood Sculpture & Frames by Kiyoshi Davis
Celtic Bas Relief by Suzuko Davis
Beadwork by Lisa Barile Knox
Photography by Mark Luttrell
Calligraphy by Sheila Hamanaka

Grandparents Song • Copyright © 2003 by Sheila Hamanaka • Manufactured in China. All rights reserved. • www.harperchildrens.com
Library of Congress Cataloging-in-Publication Data • Hamanaka, Sheila. • Grandparents song / by Sheila Hamanaka. • p.   cm.
Summary: A rhyming celebration of ancestry and of the diversity that flourishes in this country.
ISBN 0-688-17852-9— ISBN 0-688-17853-7 (lib. bdg.) • [1. Grandparents—Fiction.   2. Ethnicity—Fiction.   3. Multiculturalism—
Fiction.   4. Stories in rhyme.] I. Title. • PZ8.3.H17 Gr 2003 • 00-047952 • [E]—dc21 • 1 2 3 4 5 6 7 8 9 10
❖
First Edition

To Our
American
Ancestors
In Whose
Dreams
We Walk

My eyes are green like the sea, like the se

nd my hair is dark and blows free, blows free

I reach for the sky

like a tree, like a tree

and my roots run deep

earth is sweet, earth is sweet

Mother says she came

from the West, from the West

where the trees talk to heaven

and the spotted owls nest

And her mother came

eyes of black, eyes of black

on an Appaloosa horse

with a broad, strong back

Grandma said she came

from the earth, from the earth

that Freedom was water

and she had a great thirst

She married a man

eyes of green, eyes of green

who had left his own pony

'cross the cold northern sea

He brought a canary

and it sang of his dreams

a railroad worker

since he was fourteen

Father says he came from the South, from the South

where the scent of magnolia lulls the cottonmouth

And his mother came

eyes of black, eyes of black

across the Rio Grande

on a jaguar's back

Grandma said

from the sun

that Freedom

and her heart

she came

from the   sun

was music

was   a   drum

She married a man

eyes of night, eyes of night

and they turned the rich earth

in the dawn's early light

Grandfather's people

had crossed the great sea

Their bodies were chained

but their souls fought free

From the four directions my grandparents came

Their lives are a river that flows through my veins

My eyes are green

like the sea, like the sea

My bones are the mountains

my hair is the trees

Yes, my eyes are green like the sea, like the sea

and my hair is dark and blows free, blows free

My hair is dark and blows free